MW00902267

This book belongs to:

_____

Copyright 2019 ©

All rights reserved. No part of this publication may be copied, reproduced in any format, by any means, electronic or otherwise, without prior consent from the copywrite owner and publisher of this book.

How to use this Prayer Journal

This is a 60-day prayer journal and can be utilized to explore God's word surrounding different aspects of your life.

How to enjoy the book, Step by Step:

- You will find a list of subjects and corresponding Bible verses on the next page (page 3).

- Each day, select a verse.

- Place a check mark in the circle next to the verse you select indicating that you have completed your studies of the verse

- You will find a space at the top of each day's page to write in the verse that you selected for that day.

- Follow the prompts provided.

HOPE

- ○ Hebrews 11:11
- ○ Isaiah 40:31
- ○ Jeremiah 29:11
- ○ Romans 5:5
- ○ Romans 15:13
- ○ Romans 8:24-25
- ○ 2 Corinthians 4:17-18

FAITH

- ○ Hebrews 11:1
- ○ Matthew 21:22
- ○ Romans 10:17
- ○ Mark 11:22-24
- ○ 1 Corinthians 2:5
- ○ Luke 1:37
- ○ 2 Corinthians 5:7

DEPRESSION

- ○ Psalm 30:11
- ○ Psalm 3:3
- ○ Philippians 4:13
- ○ Matthew 11:28
- ○ Psalm 143:7-8
- ○ Psalm 23:4
- ○ Psalm 9:9

PATIENCE

- ○ Ephesians 4:2
- ○ Proverbs 16:32
- ○ Psalm 37:7
- ○ Psalm 27:14
- ○ Psalm 5:3
- ○ 2 Peter 3:8
- ○ James 5:8

FEAR

- ○ Luke 12:22-26
- ○ Psalm 55:22
- ○ Deuteronomy 31:6
- ○ Psalm 46:1
- ○ Psalm 118:6-7
- ○ Psalm 34:4
- ○ Psalm 56:3

ASHAMED

- ○ Isaiah 50:7
- ○ Philippians 1:20
- ○ Psalm 25:20
- ○ Psalm 31:1
- ○ 1 Peter 4:16
- ○ 2 Timothy 2:15
- ○ Matthew 5:15

LONELINESS

- ○ Psalm 25:16
- ○ Matthew 28:20
- ○ Isaiah 41:10
- ○ 1 Peter 5:7
- ○ Psalm 147:3
- ○ John 16:32-33

ANGER

- ○ Ephesians 4:26-31
- ○ James 1:19-20
- ○ Proverbs 29:11
- ○ Ecclesiastes 7:9
- ○ Proverbs 15:18
- ○ Proverbs 10:12

ENCOURAGEMENT

- ○ John 14:27
- ○ Psalm 34:10
- ○ Isaiah 49:13
- ○ Psalm 31:24
- ○ John 14:27
- ○ Joshua 1:9

Today's Date:_____

Let God speak to you through his Word. Select a scripture from Page 3.

Scripture selected:_____

Write down the scripture:

Study the scripture, then pray and answer the following.

Write down how you're feeling about the topic of the scripture:

_____

_____

_____

_____

What's your prayer to God surrounding the scripture?

_____

_____

_____

_____

Other Prayer Requests:

_____   _____

_____   _____

_____   _____

_____   _____

Answered Prayer Requests:

_____   _____

_____   _____

_____   _____

_____   _____

Today I am most thankful for:

_____

_____

_____

_____

Today's Date:_____

Let God speak to you through his Word. Select a scripture from Page 3.

Scripture selected:_____

Write down the scripture:

Study the scripture, then pray and answer the following.

Write down how you're feeling about the topic of the scripture:

_____

_____

_____

_____

What's your prayer to God surrounding the scripture?

_____

_____

_____

_____

Other Prayer Requests:

_____   _____

_____   _____

_____   _____

_____   _____

Answered Prayer Requests:

_____   _____

_____   _____

_____   _____

_____   _____

Today I am most thankful for:

_____

_____

_____

_____

Today's Date:_____

Let God speak to you through his Word. Select a scripture from Page 3.

Scripture selected:_____

Write down the scripture:

Study the scripture, then pray and answer the following.

Write down how you're feeling about the topic of the scripture:

_____

_____

_____

_____

What's your prayer to God surrounding the scripture?

_____

_____

_____

_____

Other Prayer Requests:

_____   _____

_____   _____

_____   _____

_____   _____

Answered Prayer Requests:

_____   _____

_____   _____

_____   _____

_____   _____

Today I am most thankful for:

_____

_____

_____

_____

Today's Date:_____

Let God speak to you through his Word. Select a scripture from Page 3.

Scripture selected:_____

Write down the scripture:

Study the scripture, then pray and answer the following.

Write down how you're feeling about the topic of the scripture:

_____

_____

_____

_____

What's your prayer to God surrounding the scripture?

_____

_____

_____

_____

Other Prayer Requests:

_____   _____

_____   _____

_____   _____

_____   _____

Answered Prayer Requests:

_____   _____

_____   _____

_____   _____

_____   _____

Today I am most thankful for:

_____

_____

_____

_____

Today's Date:_____

Let God speak to you through his Word. Select a scripture from Page 3.

Scripture selected:_____

Write down the scripture:

Study the scripture, then pray and answer the following.

Write down how you're feeling about the topic of the scripture:

_____

_____

_____

_____

What's your prayer to God surrounding the scripture?

_____

_____

_____

_____

Other Prayer Requests:

_____   _____

_____   _____

_____   _____

_____   _____

Answered Prayer Requests:

_____   _____

_____   _____

_____   _____

_____   _____

Today I am most thankful for:

_____

_____

_____

_____

Today's Date:_____

Let God speak to you through his Word. Select a scripture from Page 3.

Scripture selected:_____

Write down the scripture:

Study the scripture, then pray and answer the following.

Write down how you're feeling about the topic of the scripture:

_____

_____

_____

_____

What's your prayer to God surrounding the scripture?

_____

_____

_____

_____

Other Prayer Requests:

_____   _____

_____   _____

_____   _____

_____   _____

Answered Prayer Requests:

_____   _____

_____   _____

_____   _____

_____   _____

Today I am most thankful for:

_____

_____

_____

_____

Today's Date:_____

Let God speak to you through his Word. Select a scripture from Page 3.

Scripture selected:_____

Write down the scripture:

Study the scripture, then pray and answer the following.

Write down how you're feeling about the topic of the scripture:

_____

_____

_____

_____

What's your prayer to God surrounding the scripture?

_____

_____

_____

_____

Other Prayer Requests:

_____   _____

_____   _____

_____   _____

_____   _____

Answered Prayer Requests:

_____   _____

_____   _____

_____   _____

_____   _____

Today I am most thankful for:

_____

_____

_____

_____

Today's Date:_____

Let God speak to you through his Word. Select a scripture from Page 3.

Scripture selected:_____

Write down the scripture:

Study the scripture, then pray and answer the following.

Write down how you're feeling about the topic of the scripture:

_____

_____

_____

_____

What's your prayer to God surrounding the scripture?

_____

_____

_____

_____

Other Prayer Requests:

_____   _____

_____   _____

_____   _____

_____   _____

Answered Prayer Requests:

_____   _____

_____   _____

_____   _____

_____   _____

Today I am most thankful for:

_____

_____

_____

_____

Today's Date:_____

Let God speak to you through his Word. Select a scripture from Page 3.

Scripture selected:_____

Write down the scripture:

Study the scripture, then pray and answer the following.

Write down how you're feeling about the topic of the scripture:

_____

_____

_____

_____

What's your prayer to God surrounding the scripture?

_____

_____

_____

_____

Other Prayer Requests:

_____   _____

_____   _____

_____   _____

_____   _____

Answered Prayer Requests:

_____   _____

_____   _____

_____   _____

_____   _____

Today I am most thankful for:

_____

_____

_____

_____

Today's Date:_____

Let God speak to you through his Word. Select a scripture from Page 3.

Scripture selected:_____

Write down the scripture:

Study the scripture, then pray and answer the following.

Write down how you're feeling about the topic of the scripture:

_____

_____

_____

_____

What's your prayer to God surrounding the scripture?

_____

_____

_____

_____

Other Prayer Requests:

_____   _____

_____   _____

_____   _____

_____   _____

Answered Prayer Requests:

_____   _____

_____   _____

_____   _____

_____   _____

Today I am most thankful for:

_____

_____

_____

_____

Today's Date:_____

Let God speak to you through his Word. Select a scripture from Page 3.

Scripture selected:_____

Write down the scripture:

Study the scripture, then pray and answer the following.

Write down how you're feeling about the topic of the scripture:

_____

_____

_____

_____

What's your prayer to God surrounding the scripture?

_____

_____

_____

_____

Other Prayer Requests:

_____   _____

_____   _____

_____   _____

_____   _____

Answered Prayer Requests:

_____   _____

_____   _____

_____   _____

_____   _____

Today I am most thankful for:

_____

_____

_____

_____

Today's Date:_____

Let God speak to you through his Word. Select a scripture from Page 3.

Scripture selected:_____

Write down the scripture:

Study the scripture, then pray and answer the following.

Write down how you're feeling about the topic of the scripture:

_____

_____

_____

_____

What's your prayer to God surrounding the scripture?

_____

_____

_____

_____

Other Prayer Requests:

_____   _____

_____   _____

_____   _____

_____   _____

Answered Prayer Requests:

_____   _____

_____   _____

_____   _____

_____   _____

Today I am most thankful for:

_____

_____

_____

_____

Today's Date:_____

Let God speak to you through his Word. Select a scripture from Page 3.

Scripture selected:_____

Write down the scripture:

Study the scripture, then pray and answer the following.

Write down how you're feeling about the topic of the scripture:

_____

_____

_____

_____

What's your prayer to God surrounding the scripture?

_____

_____

_____

_____

Other Prayer Requests:

_____   _____

_____   _____

_____   _____

_____   _____

Answered Prayer Requests:

_____   _____

_____   _____

_____   _____

_____   _____

Today I am most thankful for:

_____

_____

_____

_____

Today's Date:_____

Let God speak to you through his Word. Select a scripture from Page 3.

Scripture selected:_____

Write down the scripture:

Study the scripture, then pray and answer the following.

Write down how you're feeling about the topic of the scripture:

_____

_____

_____

_____

What's your prayer to God surrounding the scripture?

_____

_____

_____

_____

Other Prayer Requests:

_____   _____

_____   _____

_____   _____

_____   _____

Answered Prayer Requests:

_____   _____

_____   _____

_____   _____

_____   _____

Today I am most thankful for:

_____

_____

_____

_____

Today's Date:_____

Let God speak to you through his Word. Select a scripture from Page 3.

Scripture selected:_____

Write down the scripture:

Study the scripture, then pray and answer the following.

Write down how you're feeling about the topic of the scripture:

_____

_____

_____

_____

What's your prayer to God surrounding the scripture?

_____

_____

_____

_____

Other Prayer Requests:

_____   _____

_____   _____

_____   _____

_____   _____

Answered Prayer Requests:

_____   _____

_____   _____

_____   _____

_____   _____

Today I am most thankful for:

_____

_____

_____

_____

Today's Date:_____

Let God speak to you through his Word. Select a scripture from Page 3.

Scripture selected:_____

Write down the scripture:

Study the scripture, then pray and answer the following.

Write down how you're feeling about the topic of the scripture:

_____

_____

_____

_____

What's your prayer to God surrounding the scripture?

_____

_____

_____

_____

Other Prayer Requests:

_____   _____

_____   _____

_____   _____

_____   _____

Answered Prayer Requests:

_____   _____

_____   _____

_____   _____

_____   _____

Today I am most thankful for:

_____

_____

_____

_____

Today's Date:_____

Let God speak to you through his Word. Select a scripture from Page 3.

Scripture selected:_____

Write down the scripture:

Study the scripture, then pray and answer the following.

Write down how you're feeling about the topic of the scripture:

_____

_____

_____

_____

What's your prayer to God surrounding the scripture?

_____

_____

_____

_____

Other Prayer Requests:

_____   _____

_____   _____

_____   _____

_____   _____

Answered Prayer Requests:

_____   _____

_____   _____

_____   _____

_____   _____

Today I am most thankful for:

_____

_____

_____

_____

Today's Date:_____

Let God speak to you through his Word. Select a scripture from Page 3.

Scripture selected:_____

Write down the scripture:

Study the scripture, then pray and answer the following.

Write down how you're feeling about the topic of the scripture:

_____

_____

_____

_____

What's your prayer to God surrounding the scripture?

_____

_____

_____

_____

Other Prayer Requests:

_____   _____

_____   _____

_____   _____

_____   _____

Answered Prayer Requests:

_____   _____

_____   _____

_____   _____

_____   _____

Today I am most thankful for:

_____

_____

_____

_____

Today's Date:_____

Let God speak to you through his Word. Select a scripture from Page 3.

Scripture selected:_____

Write down the scripture:

Study the scripture, then pray and answer the following.

Write down how you're feeling about the topic of the scripture:

_____

_____

_____

_____

What's your prayer to God surrounding the scripture?

_____

_____

_____

_____

Other Prayer Requests:

_____ _____

_____ _____

_____ _____

_____ _____

Answered Prayer Requests:

_____ _____

_____ _____

_____ _____

_____ _____

Today I am most thankful for:

_____

_____

_____

_____

Today's Date:_____

Let God speak to you through his Word. Select a scripture from Page 3.

Scripture selected:_____

Write down the scripture:

Study the scripture, then pray and answer the following.

Write down how you're feeling about the topic of the scripture:

_____

_____

_____

_____

What's your prayer to God surrounding the scripture?

_____

_____

_____

_____

Other Prayer Requests:

_____   _____

_____   _____

_____   _____

_____   _____

Answered Prayer Requests:

_____   _____

_____   _____

_____   _____

_____   _____

Today I am most thankful for:

_____

_____

_____

_____

Today's Date:_____

Let God speak to you through his Word. Select a scripture from Page 3.

Scripture selected:_____

Write down the scripture:

Study the scripture, then pray and answer the following.

Write down how you're feeling about the topic of the scripture:

_____

_____

_____

_____

What's your prayer to God surrounding the scripture?

_____

_____

_____

_____

Other Prayer Requests:

_____   _____

_____   _____

_____   _____

_____   _____

Answered Prayer Requests:

_____   _____

_____   _____

_____   _____

_____   _____

Today I am most thankful for:

_____

_____

_____

_____

Today's Date:_____

Let God speak to you through his Word. Select a scripture from Page 3.

Scripture selected:_____

Write down the scripture:

Study the scripture, then pray and answer the following.

Write down how you're feeling about the topic of the scripture:

_____

_____

_____

_____

What's your prayer to God surrounding the scripture?

_____

_____

_____

_____

Other Prayer Requests:

_____ _____

_____ _____

_____ _____

_____ _____

Answered Prayer Requests:

_____ _____

_____ _____

_____ _____

_____ _____

Today I am most thankful for:

_____

_____

_____

_____

Today's Date:_____

Let God speak to you through his Word. Select a scripture from Page 3.

Scripture selected:_____

Write down the scripture:

Study the scripture, then pray and answer the following.

Write down how you're feeling about the topic of the scripture:

_____

_____

_____

_____

What's your prayer to God surrounding the scripture?

_____

_____

_____

_____

Other Prayer Requests:

_____   _____

_____   _____

_____   _____

_____   _____

Answered Prayer Requests:

_____   _____

_____   _____

_____   _____

_____   _____

Today I am most thankful for:

_____

_____

_____

_____

Today's Date:_____

Let God speak to you through his Word. Select a scripture from Page 3.

Scripture selected:_____

Write down the scripture:

Study the scripture, then pray and answer the following.

Write down how you're feeling about the topic of the scripture:

_____

_____

_____

_____

What's your prayer to God surrounding the scripture?

_____

_____

_____

_____

Other Prayer Requests:

_____ _____

_____ _____

_____ _____

_____ _____

Answered Prayer Requests:

_____ _____

_____ _____

_____ _____

_____ _____

Today I am most thankful for:

_____

_____

_____

_____

Today's Date:_____

Let God speak to you through his Word. Select a scripture from Page 3.

Scripture selected:_____

Write down the scripture:

Study the scripture, then pray and answer the following.

Write down how you're feeling about the topic of the scripture:

_____

_____

_____

_____

What's your prayer to God surrounding the scripture?

_____

_____

_____

_____

Other Prayer Requests:

_____   _____

_____   _____

_____   _____

_____   _____

Answered Prayer Requests:

_____   _____

_____   _____

_____   _____

_____   _____

Today I am most thankful for:

_____

_____

_____

_____

Today's Date:_____

Let God speak to you through his Word. Select a scripture from Page 3.

Scripture selected:_____

Write down the scripture:

Study the scripture, then pray and answer the following.

Write down how you're feeling about the topic of the scripture:

_____

_____

_____

_____

What's your prayer to God surrounding the scripture?

_____

_____

_____

_____

Other Prayer Requests:

_____   _____

_____   _____

_____   _____

_____   _____

Answered Prayer Requests:

_____   _____

_____   _____

_____   _____

_____   _____

Today I am most thankful for:

_____

_____

_____

_____

Today's Date:_____

Let God speak to you through his Word. Select a scripture from Page 3.

Scripture selected:_____

Write down the scripture:

Study the scripture, then pray and answer the following.

Write down how you're feeling about the topic of the scripture:

_____

_____

_____

_____

What's your prayer to God surrounding the scripture?

_____

_____

_____

_____

Other Prayer Requests:

_____   _____

_____   _____

_____   _____

_____   _____

Answered Prayer Requests:

_____   _____

_____   _____

_____   _____

_____   _____

Today I am most thankful for:

_____

_____

_____

_____

Today's Date:_____

Let God speak to you through his Word. Select a scripture from Page 3.

Scripture selected:_____

Write down the scripture:

Study the scripture, then pray and answer the following.

Write down how you're feeling about the topic of the scripture:

_____

_____

_____

_____

What's your prayer to God surrounding the scripture?

_____

_____

_____

_____

Other Prayer Requests:

_____   _____

_____   _____

_____   _____

_____   _____

Answered Prayer Requests:

_____   _____

_____   _____

_____   _____

_____   _____

Today I am most thankful for:

_____

_____

_____

_____

Today's Date:_____

Let God speak to you through his Word. Select a scripture from Page 3.

Scripture selected:_____

Write down the scripture:

Study the scripture, then pray and answer the following.

Write down how you're feeling about the topic of the scripture:

_____

_____

_____

_____

What's your prayer to God surrounding the scripture?

_____

_____

_____

_____

Other Prayer Requests:

_____   _____

_____   _____

_____   _____

_____   _____

Answered Prayer Requests:

_____   _____

_____   _____

_____   _____

_____   _____

Today I am most thankful for:

_____

_____

_____

_____

Today's Date:_____

Let God speak to you through his Word. Select a scripture from Page 3.

Scripture selected:_____

Write down the scripture:

Study the scripture, then pray and answer the following.

Write down how you're feeling about the topic of the scripture:

_____

_____

_____

_____

What's your prayer to God surrounding the scripture?

_____

_____

_____

_____

Other Prayer Requests:

_____   _____

_____   _____

_____   _____

_____   _____

Answered Prayer Requests:

_____   _____

_____   _____

_____   _____

_____   _____

Today I am most thankful for:

_____

_____

_____

_____

Today's Date:_____

Let God speak to you through his Word. Select a scripture from Page 3.

Scripture selected:_____

Write down the scripture:

Study the scripture, then pray and answer the following.

Write down how you're feeling about the topic of the scripture:

_____

_____

_____

_____

What's your prayer to God surrounding the scripture?

_____

_____

_____

_____

Other Prayer Requests:

_____   _____

_____   _____

_____   _____

_____   _____

Answered Prayer Requests:

_____   _____

_____   _____

_____   _____

_____   _____

Today I am most thankful for:

_____

_____

_____

_____

Today's Date:_____

Let God speak to you through his Word. Select a scripture from Page 3.

Scripture selected:_____

Write down the scripture:

Study the scripture, then pray and answer the following.

❧ ❧ ❧ ❧ ❧ ❧ ❧

Write down how you're feeling about the topic of the scripture:

_____

_____

_____

_____

❧ ❧ ❧ ❧ ❧ ❧ ❧

What's your prayer to God surrounding the scripture?

_____

_____

_____

_____

Other Prayer Requests:

_____   _____

_____   _____

_____   _____

_____   _____

Answered Prayer Requests:

_____   _____

_____   _____

_____   _____

_____   _____

Today I am most thankful for:

_____

_____

_____

_____

Today's Date:_____

Let God speak to you through his Word. Select a scripture from Page 3.

Scripture selected:_____

Write down the scripture:

Study the scripture, then pray and answer the following.

Write down how you're feeling about the topic of the scripture:

_____

_____

_____

_____

What's your prayer to God surrounding the scripture?

_____

_____

_____

_____

Other Prayer Requests:

_____   _____

_____   _____

_____   _____

_____   _____

Answered Prayer Requests:

_____   _____

_____   _____

_____   _____

_____   _____

Today I am most thankful for:

_____

_____

_____

_____

Today's Date:_____

Let God speak to you through his Word. Select a scripture from Page 3.

Scripture selected:_____

Write down the scripture:

Study the scripture, then pray and answer the following.

Write down how you're feeling about the topic of the scripture:

_____

_____

_____

_____

What's your prayer to God surrounding the scripture?

_____

_____

_____

_____

Other Prayer Requests:

_____ _____

_____ _____

_____ _____

_____ _____

Answered Prayer Requests:

_____ _____

_____ _____

_____ _____

_____ _____

Today I am most thankful for:

_____

_____

_____

_____

Today's Date:_____

Let God speak to you through his Word. Select a scripture from Page 3.

Scripture selected:_____

Write down the scripture:

Study the scripture, then pray and answer the following.

Write down how you're feeling about the topic of the scripture:

_____

_____

_____

_____

What's your prayer to God surrounding the scripture?

_____

_____

_____

_____

Other Prayer Requests:

_____   _____

_____   _____

_____   _____

_____   _____

Answered Prayer Requests:

_____   _____

_____   _____

_____   _____

_____   _____

Today I am most thankful for:

_____

_____

_____

_____

Today's Date:_____

Let God speak to you through his Word. Select a scripture from Page 3.

Scripture selected:_____

Write down the scripture:

Study the scripture, then pray and answer the following.

Write down how you're feeling about the topic of the scripture:

_____

_____

_____

_____

What's your prayer to God surrounding the scripture?

_____

_____

_____

_____

Other Prayer Requests:

_____   _____

_____   _____

_____   _____

_____   _____

Answered Prayer Requests:

_____   _____

_____   _____

_____   _____

_____   _____

Today I am most thankful for:

_____

_____

_____

_____

Today's Date:_____

Let God speak to you through his Word. Select a scripture from Page 3.

Scripture selected:_____

Write down the scripture:

Study the scripture, then pray and answer the following.

Write down how you're feeling about the topic of the scripture:

_____

_____

_____

_____

What's your prayer to God surrounding the scripture?

_____

_____

_____

_____

Other Prayer Requests:

_____   _____

_____   _____

_____   _____

_____   _____

Answered Prayer Requests:

_____   _____

_____   _____

_____   _____

_____   _____

Today I am most thankful for:

_____

_____

_____

_____

Today's Date:_____

Let God speak to you through his Word. Select a scripture from Page 3.

Scripture selected:_____

Write down the scripture:

Study the scripture, then pray and answer the following.

Write down how you're feeling about the topic of the scripture:

_____

_____

_____

_____

What's your prayer to God surrounding the scripture?

_____

_____

_____

_____

Other Prayer Requests:

_____   _____

_____   _____

_____   _____

_____   _____

Answered Prayer Requests:

_____   _____

_____   _____

_____   _____

_____   _____

Today I am most thankful for:

_____

_____

_____

_____

Today's Date:_____

Let God speak to you through his Word. Select a scripture from Page 3.

Scripture selected:_____

Write down the scripture:

Study the scripture, then pray and answer the following.

Write down how you're feeling about the topic of the scripture:

_____

_____

_____

_____

What's your prayer to God surrounding the scripture?

_____

_____

_____

_____

Other Prayer Requests:

_____   _____

_____   _____

_____   _____

_____   _____

Answered Prayer Requests:

_____   _____

_____   _____

_____   _____

_____   _____

Today I am most thankful for:

_____

_____

_____

_____

Today's Date:_____

Let God speak to you through his Word. Select a scripture from Page 3.

Scripture selected:_____

Write down the scripture:

Study the scripture, then pray and answer the following.

Write down how you're feeling about the topic of the scripture:

_____

_____

_____

_____

What's your prayer to God surrounding the scripture?

_____

_____

_____

_____

Other Prayer Requests:

_____   _____

_____   _____

_____   _____

_____   _____

Answered Prayer Requests:

_____   _____

_____   _____

_____   _____

_____   _____

Today I am most thankful for:

_____

_____

_____

_____

Today's Date:_____

Let God speak to you through his Word. Select a scripture from Page 3.

Scripture selected:_____

Write down the scripture:

Study the scripture, then pray and answer the following.

Write down how you're feeling about the topic of the scripture:

_____

_____

_____

_____

What's your prayer to God surrounding the scripture?

_____

_____

_____

_____

Other Prayer Requests:

_____   _____

_____   _____

_____   _____

_____   _____

Answered Prayer Requests:

_____   _____

_____   _____

_____   _____

_____   _____

Today I am most thankful for:

_____

_____

_____

_____

Today's Date:_____

Let God speak to you through his Word. Select a scripture from Page 3.

Scripture selected:_____

Write down the scripture:

Study the scripture, then pray and answer the following.

Write down how you're feeling about the topic of the scripture:

_____

_____

_____

_____

What's your prayer to God surrounding the scripture?

_____

_____

_____

_____

Other Prayer Requests:

_____   _____

_____   _____

_____   _____

_____   _____

Answered Prayer Requests:

_____   _____

_____   _____

_____   _____

_____   _____

Today I am most thankful for:

_____

_____

_____

_____

Today's Date:_____

Let God speak to you through his Word. Select a scripture from Page 3.

Scripture selected:_____

Write down the scripture:

Study the scripture, then pray and answer the following.

Write down how you're feeling about the topic of the scripture:

_____

_____

_____

_____

What's your prayer to God surrounding the scripture?

_____

_____

_____

_____

Other Prayer Requests:

_____   _____

_____   _____

_____   _____

_____   _____

Answered Prayer Requests:

_____   _____

_____   _____

_____   _____

_____   _____

Today I am most thankful for:

_____

_____

_____

_____

Today's Date:_____

Let God speak to you through his Word. Select a scripture from Page 3.

Scripture selected:_____

Write down the scripture:

Study the scripture, then pray and answer the following.

Write down how you're feeling about the topic of the scripture:

_____

_____

_____

_____

What's your prayer to God surrounding the scripture?

_____

_____

_____

_____

Other Prayer Requests:

_____   _____

_____   _____

_____   _____

_____   _____

Answered Prayer Requests:

_____   _____

_____   _____

_____   _____

_____   _____

Today I am most thankful for:

_____

_____

_____

_____

Today's Date:_____

Let God speak to you through his Word. Select a scripture from Page 3.

Scripture selected:_____

Write down the scripture:

Study the scripture, then pray and answer the following.

Write down how you're feeling about the topic of the scripture:

_____

_____

_____

_____

What's your prayer to God surrounding the scripture?

_____

_____

_____

_____

Other Prayer Requests:

_____   _____

_____   _____

_____   _____

_____   _____

Answered Prayer Requests:

_____   _____

_____   _____

_____   _____

_____   _____

Today I am most thankful for:

_____

_____

_____

_____

Today's Date:_____

Let God speak to you through his Word. Select a scripture from Page 3.

Scripture selected:_____

Write down the scripture:

Study the scripture, then pray and answer the following.

Write down how you're feeling about the topic of the scripture:

_____

_____

_____

_____

What's your prayer to God surrounding the scripture?

_____

_____

_____

_____

Other Prayer Requests:

_____   _____

_____   _____

_____   _____

_____   _____

Answered Prayer Requests:

_____   _____

_____   _____

_____   _____

_____   _____

Today I am most thankful for:

_____

_____

_____

_____

Today's Date:_____

Let God speak to you through his Word. Select a scripture from Page 3.

Scripture selected:_____

Write down the scripture:

Study the scripture, then pray and answer the following.

Write down how you're feeling about the topic of the scripture:

_____

_____

_____

_____

What's your prayer to God surrounding the scripture?

_____

_____

_____

_____

Other Prayer Requests:

_____   _____

_____   _____

_____   _____

_____   _____

Answered Prayer Requests:

_____   _____

_____   _____

_____   _____

_____   _____

Today I am most thankful for:

_____

_____

_____

_____

Today's Date:_____

Let God speak to you through his Word. Select a scripture from Page 3.

Scripture selected:_____

Write down the scripture:

Study the scripture, then pray and answer the following.

Write down how you're feeling about the topic of the scripture:

_____

_____

_____

_____

What's your prayer to God surrounding the scripture?

_____

_____

_____

_____

Other Prayer Requests:

_____   _____

_____   _____

_____   _____

_____   _____

Answered Prayer Requests:

_____   _____

_____   _____

_____   _____

_____   _____

Today I am most thankful for:

_____

_____

_____

_____

Today's Date:_____

Let God speak to you through his Word. Select a scripture from Page 3.

Scripture selected:_____

Write down the scripture:

Study the scripture, then pray and answer the following.

Write down how you're feeling about the topic of the scripture:

_____

_____

_____

_____

What's your prayer to God surrounding the scripture?

_____

_____

_____

_____

Other Prayer Requests:

_____   _____

_____   _____

_____   _____

_____   _____

Answered Prayer Requests:

_____   _____

_____   _____

_____   _____

_____   _____

Today I am most thankful for:

_____

_____

_____

_____

Today's Date:_____

Let God speak to you through his Word. Select a scripture from Page 3.

Scripture selected:_____

Write down the scripture:

Study the scripture, then pray and answer the following.

Write down how you're feeling about the topic of the scripture:

_____

_____

_____

_____

What's your prayer to God surrounding the scripture?

_____

_____

_____

_____

Other Prayer Requests:

_____   _____

_____   _____

_____   _____

_____   _____

Answered Prayer Requests:

_____   _____

_____   _____

_____   _____

_____   _____

Today I am most thankful for:

_____

_____

_____

_____

Today's Date:_____

Let God speak to you through his Word. Select a scripture from Page 3.

Scripture selected:_____

Write down the scripture:

Study the scripture, then pray and answer the following.

Write down how you're feeling about the topic of the scripture:

_____

_____

_____

_____

What's your prayer to God surrounding the scripture?

_____

_____

_____

_____

Other Prayer Requests:

_____ _____

_____ _____

_____ _____

_____ _____

Answered Prayer Requests:

_____ _____

_____ _____

_____ _____

_____ _____

Today I am most thankful for:

_____

_____

_____

_____

Today's Date:_____

Let God speak to you through his Word. Select a scripture from Page 3.

Scripture selected:_____

Write down the scripture:

Study the scripture, then pray and answer the following.

Write down how you're feeling about the topic of the scripture:

_____

_____

_____

_____

What's your prayer to God surrounding the scripture?

_____

_____

_____

_____

Other Prayer Requests:

_____   _____

_____   _____

_____   _____

_____   _____

Answered Prayer Requests:

_____   _____

_____   _____

_____   _____

_____   _____

Today I am most thankful for:

_____

_____

_____

_____

Today's Date:_____

Let God speak to you through his Word. Select a scripture from Page 3.

Scripture selected:_____

Write down the scripture:

Study the scripture, then pray and answer the following.

Write down how you're feeling about the topic of the scripture:

_____

_____

_____

_____

What's your prayer to God surrounding the scripture?

_____

_____

_____

_____

Other Prayer Requests:

_____   _____

_____   _____

_____   _____

_____   _____

Answered Prayer Requests:

_____   _____

_____   _____

_____   _____

_____   _____

Today I am most thankful for:

_____

_____

_____

_____

Today's Date:_____

Let God speak to you through his Word. Select a scripture from Page 3.

Scripture selected:_____

Write down the scripture:

Study the scripture, then pray and answer the following.

Write down how you're feeling about the topic of the scripture:

_____

_____

_____

_____

What's your prayer to God surrounding the scripture?

_____

_____

_____

_____

Other Prayer Requests:

_____   _____

_____   _____

_____   _____

_____   _____

Answered Prayer Requests:

_____   _____

_____   _____

_____   _____

_____   _____

Today I am most thankful for:

_____

_____

_____

_____

Today's Date:_____

Let God speak to you through his Word. Select a scripture from Page 3.

Scripture selected:_____

Write down the scripture:

Study the scripture, then pray and answer the following.

Write down how you're feeling about the topic of the scripture:

_____

_____

_____

_____

What's your prayer to God surrounding the scripture?

_____

_____

_____

_____

Other Prayer Requests:

_____   _____

_____   _____

_____   _____

_____   _____

Answered Prayer Requests:

_____   _____

_____   _____

_____   _____

_____   _____

Today I am most thankful for:

_____

_____

_____

_____

Today's Date:_____

Let God speak to you through his Word. Select a scripture from Page 3.

Scripture selected:_____

Write down the scripture:

Study the scripture, then pray and answer the following.

Write down how you're feeling about the topic of the scripture:

_____

_____

_____

_____

What's your prayer to God surrounding the scripture?

_____

_____

_____

_____

Other Prayer Requests:

_____   _____

_____   _____

_____   _____

_____   _____

Answered Prayer Requests:

_____   _____

_____   _____

_____   _____

_____   _____

Today I am most thankful for:

_____

_____

_____

_____

Today's Date:_____

Let God speak to you through his Word. Select a scripture from Page 3.

Scripture selected:_____

Write down the scripture:

Study the scripture, then pray and answer the following.

Write down how you're feeling about the topic of the scripture:

_____

_____

_____

_____

What's your prayer to God surrounding the scripture?

_____

_____

_____

_____

Other Prayer Requests:

_____   _____

_____   _____

_____   _____

_____   _____

Answered Prayer Requests:

_____   _____

_____   _____

_____   _____

_____   _____

Today I am most thankful for:

_____

_____

_____

_____

Today's Date:_____

Let God speak to you through his Word. Select a scripture from Page 3.

Scripture selected:_____

Write down the scripture:

Study the scripture, then pray and answer the following.

Write down how you're feeling about the topic of the scripture:

_____

_____

_____

_____

What's your prayer to God surrounding the scripture?

_____

_____

_____

_____

Other Prayer Requests:

_____ _____

_____ _____

_____ _____

_____ _____

Answered Prayer Requests:

_____ _____

_____ _____

_____ _____

_____ _____

Today I am most thankful for:

_____

_____

_____

_____

Today's Date:_____

Let God speak to you through his Word. Select a scripture from Page 3.

Scripture selected:_____

Write down the scripture:

Study the scripture, then pray and answer the following.

Write down how you're feeling about the topic of the scripture:

_____

_____

_____

_____

What's your prayer to God surrounding the scripture?

_____

_____

_____

_____

Other Prayer Requests:

_____   _____

_____   _____

_____   _____

_____   _____

Answered Prayer Requests:

_____   _____

_____   _____

_____   _____

_____   _____

Today I am most thankful for:

_____

_____

_____

_____

Today's Date:_____

Let God speak to you through his Word. Select a scripture from Page 3.

Scripture selected:_____

Write down the scripture:

Study the scripture, then pray and answer the following.

Write down how you're feeling about the topic of the scripture:

_____

_____

_____

_____

What's your prayer to God surrounding the scripture?

_____

_____

_____

_____

Other Prayer Requests:

_____   _____

_____   _____

_____   _____

_____   _____

Answered Prayer Requests:

_____   _____

_____   _____

_____   _____

_____   _____

Today I am most thankful for:

_____

_____

_____

_____

Made in the USA
Middletown, DE
18 May 2021

39921546R00068